WILDERNESS ADVENTURES

Hunting

Seth Kingston

PowerKiDS press
NEW YORK

Published in 2022 by The Rosen Publishing Group, Inc.
29 East 21st Street, New York, NY 10010

First Edition

Portions of this work were originally authored by Suzanne Slade and published as *Let's Go Hunting.* All new material in this edition was authored by Seth Kingston.

Editor: Caitie McAneney
Book Design: Michael Flynn

Photo Credits: Cover (hunter), p. 1, Tyler Stableford/Stone/Getty Images; cover, pp. 1, 7, 13, 17, 29 (mountain logo) doyz86/Shutterstock.com; interior (mountain background) Lidiia/Shutterstock.com; pp. 5, 21, 25 Mitch Kezar/Design Pics/Getty Images; p. 7 (buffalo hunt) Gift of Dr. and Mrs. John E. Larkin, Jr./Minneapolis Institute of Art; p. 7 (cheetah) Freder/E+/Getty Images; p. 8 Jason Finn/iStock/Getty Images; p. 9 JonHuelskamp/iStock/Getty Images; p. 11 chandlerphoto/E+/Getty Images; p. 12 snowflock/iStock/Getty Images; p. 13 RichLegg/E+/Getty Images; p. 14 kali9/E+/Getty Images; p. 15 ZoranOrcik/Shutterstock.com; p. 17 Jell Clow/EyeEm/Getty Images; p. 19 (deer) Larry Keller, Lititz Pa./Moment/Getty Images; p. 19 (deer stand) statu-nascendi/iStock/Getty Images; p. 20 davidsdodd/iStock/Getty Images; p. 23 Ksenia Raykova/iStock/Getty Images; p. 27 Rubberball Productions/Brand X Pictures/Getty Images; p. 28 Jordan Siemens/Stone/Getty Images; p. 29 TracieMichelle/iStock/Getty Images.

Library of Congress Cataloging-in-Publication Data

Names: Kingston, Seth, author.
Title: Hunting / Seth Kingston.
Description: New York : PowerKids Press, [2022] | Series: Wilderness adventures | Includes index.
Identifiers: LCCN 2020039474 | ISBN 9781725329393 (library binding) | ISBN 9781725329379 (paperback) | ISBN 9781725329386 (6 pack)
Subjects: LCSH: Hunting--Juvenile literature.
Classification: LCC SK35.5 .K49 2022 | DDC 639/.1--dc23
LC record available at https://lccn.loc.gov/2020039474

Manufactured in the United States of America

Some of the images in this book illustrate individuals who are models. The depictions do not imply actual situations or events.

Note to Parents and Teachers: Some of the activities in this book require adult supervision. Please talk with your child or student before allowing them to proceed with any wilderness activities.

CPSIA Compliance Information: Batch #CWPK22. For further information contact Rosen Publishing, New York, New York at 1-800-237-9932.

CONTENTS

Hunting for Sport

Hunting is one way to explore and connect with nature. Even kids can hunt, as long as they're with a skilled adult. Hunters enjoy observing wildlife. They study animals that live in different **habitats**, from deep woods to areas around lakes and streams. You can use your knowledge about animal **behavior** to help you hunt for animals.

Some people hunt for sport, or just for fun. They use skills and gear to find and hunt game, or animals. Some people stuff and display their game, while others use fur or hides to make clothes or belts. Many people hunt for food to eat. They prepare the meat and cook it for their family. Some families pass down their hunting skills to younger **generations**.

Many hunters in North America hunt deer for food and sport. Deer meat is called venison.

Hunting Throughout History

Prehistoric peoples were hunters and gatherers. They hunted animals and gathered plants, like berries, for food. They had to hunt whatever was available, and whatever they could kill without risking their own lives. Cave paintings show people hunting for animals as many as 35,000 years ago. Some animals include **ancient** pigs, monkeys, horses, and bison. Prehistoric peoples hunted these animals for food and clothing. These early hunters had to hunt to stay alive.

People developed, or created, many different hunting methods. Some hunted with spears, clubs, or sharp stone tools. Native peoples of Australia used a curved blade called a boomerang on their hunts. Native peoples of North America hunted with bows and arrows. Some rode atop horses in large bison hunts.

CHEETAHS ON THE HUNT

Throughout history, animals were sometimes used to help with hunting. Different peoples used cheetahs for hunting over hundreds of years. As a natural predator and the world's fastest land mammal, cheetahs made the perfect hunting companion. They also have great eyesight and can make sounds like a bird as a trap. Ancient Sumerians and Egyptians used cheetahs as many as 5,000 years ago. It's also said that a famous ruler in 16th-century India called Akbar owned thousands of cheetahs for hunting.

This artwork shows a member of a North American Plains tribe shooting an arrow at a bison while riding a horse.

Where Can You Hunt?

Today, you can only hunt in certain areas, and only at certain times of the year. Search for a place to hunt before you plan your trip. You might need **reservations** to hunt in certain areas, even if you're hunting close to home.

You will need a hunting **license** for your state. If you want to hunt in another state, you may need to fill out forms for that state in advance. Wherever you hunt, remember to look for and obey signs that say No Hunting.

Keep a lookout for signs that say Private Property or Public Hunting.

A hunting preserve is one of the best places to hunt. Preserves are large areas that are reserved for hunters. Many kinds of wild game live in preserves, such as deer, elk, pheasant, ducks, quail, and turkeys.

WILD FILE

If you ask permission, farmers might allow you to hunt on their private land. This can help them reduce the populations of wild animals on their land.

What Should You Wear?

When you're out in nature, you need to wear certain clothes to be comfortable and safe. Hunting can mean spending a lot of time outdoors—in the cold, heat, or other elements. Hunters must choose clothing that allows them to move quickly. Most hunters wear several layers of clothes. The outer layer is for protection from the weather. Layers of clothing may be added under the top layer for warmth.

Many states require hunters to wear a bright orange piece of clothing. This helps hunters recognize each other and prevents accidental shootings. When hunting at close range for animals such as turkeys or ducks, hunters often wear camouflage clothing. Camouflage is green and brown. It helps hunters blend into their surroundings so animals can't see them.

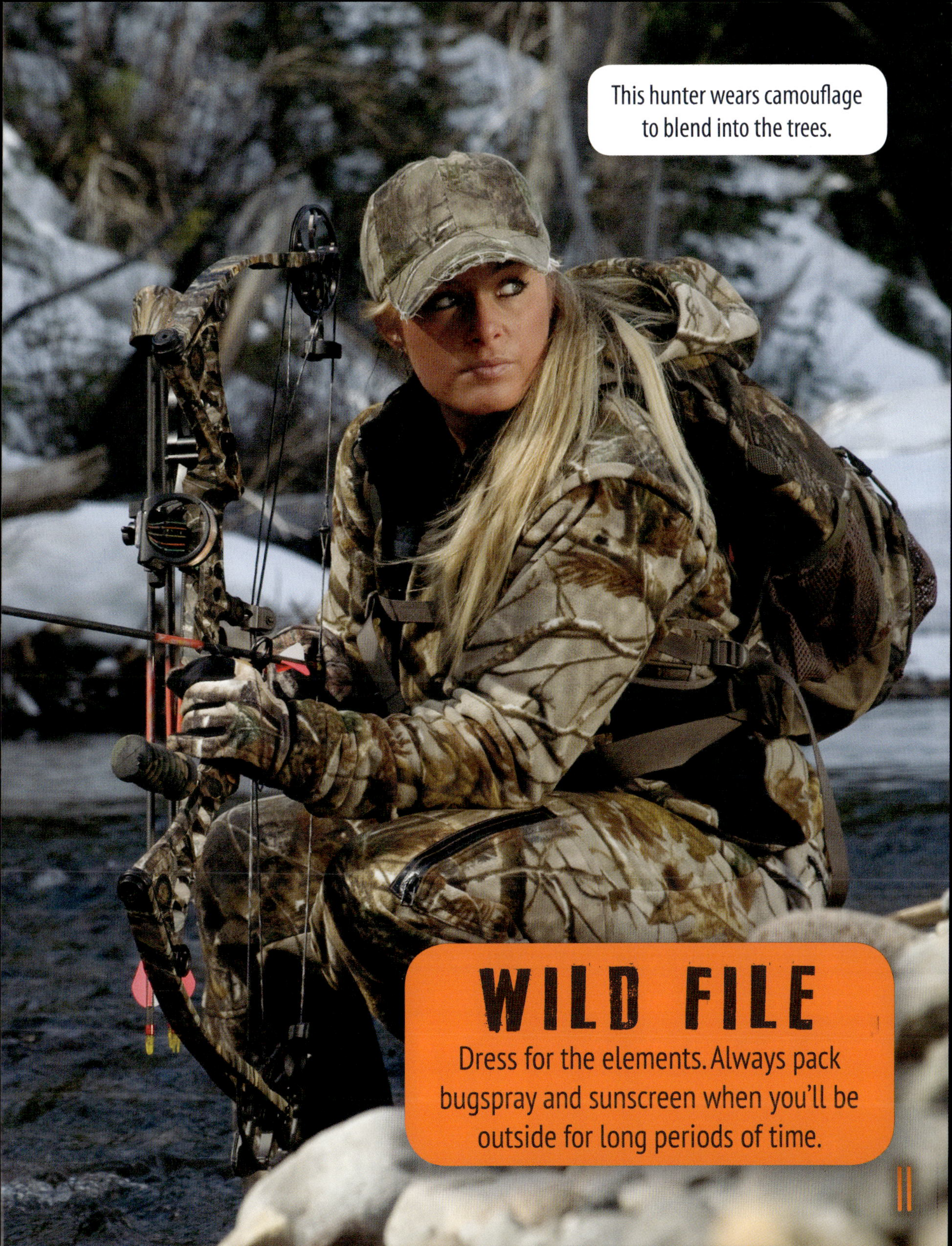

This hunter wears camouflage to blend into the trees.

WILD FILE

Dress for the elements. Always pack bugspray and sunscreen when you'll be outside for long periods of time.

Lots to Learn

You have to learn about hunting before you do it. It can be a dangerous sport if you don't know much about it. You can read books about hunting. You should also find an adult who can teach you about hunting gear and safety.

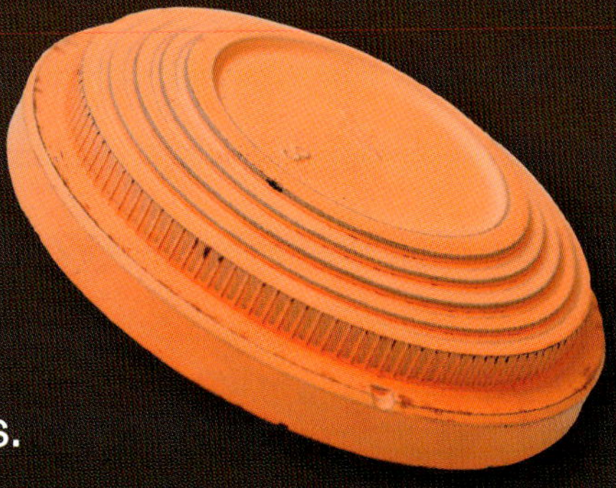

It's important to practice with your gear before you go hunting. Hunters often go to a shooting range to practice using a gun or a bow and arrows. Large targets are placed at close range for beginning shooters. More advanced shooters can aim at small targets at longer ranges. Hunters can also practice aiming at moving targets called clay pigeons at a shooting range. A machine called a trap throws the clay pigeons into the air. This can help you practice your aim and gun skills.

WILD FILE

A clay pigeon is a heavy, round disc.

GUN SAFETY

Guns can be very dangerous. You need to know how to handle a firearm before you go hunting with one. Hunters use **TABK** rules:

Treat every firearm like it's loaded.

Always point the firearm in a direction that's safe—never toward a person.

Be sure of your target. You want to make sure you are seeing your target clearly.

Keep your finger off the trigger (and out of the trigger guard) until you are ready to shoot.

Many shooting ranges have both indoor and outdoor target practice.

Different Gear

You should know what type of gun you need for the game you hope to hunt. Different guns work best for hunting different animals. For big game, such as deer or elk, hunters generally use a rifle. A rifle has a long, thin barrel and shoots a lead bullet. Hunters look through a sight or scope mounted on the rifle. This helps them take aim.

This hunter uses a shotgun.

Hunters often use a shotgun for hunting small animals. A shell is shot out of the long, fat barrel of a shotgun. The shell holds many tiny metal balls. These are called buckshot. When a shotgun is fired, it sends out pieces of buckshot over a large area. Then, there's a better chance of hitting smaller animals.

shotgun shells

Hunting Big and Small

You can either hunt big game or small game. Small game animals include rabbits, hares, squirrels, and racoons. Small game hunting is popular because small game is generally easy to find. People hunt small game for food and for sport. A new hunter might start by trying to bag, or catch, a squirrel or rabbit. These animals are especially plentiful in most areas.

Big game hunting is more of a challenge. Big game animals include deer, elk, moose, black bears, and pronghorn. Hunters sometimes walk several miles over rough ground to find big game animals. If a big game hunter is successful, the heavy animal must also be carried back.

Some places require special licenses or permissions to hunt big game.

HUNTING TAGS

For certain animals—like bears and moose—you need a special permit called a tag. Some tags can only be obtained through a **lottery** system. You can only hunt the number of animals for which you have tags. Once you **harvest** the animal, you need to attach the tag to it. Tags help wildlife experts keep track of the number of animals in an area. Then, they can keep the **ecosystem** in balance.

WILD FILE

There are usually limits to the number and kind of big game animal you can hunt.

The North American pronghorn is the second fastest mammal in the world!

Scouting

How can you locate an animal? Hunters use a special skill called scouting. First, you have to keep an eye out for clues. Hunters look for animal tracks, feeding spots, bedding areas, and scat. These clues help hunters know what kinds of animals are nearby.

When a hunter finds an animal, they must decide whether to stalk hunt or stand hunt. Stalk hunting is useful when a hunter sees an animal that is far away. A stalk hunter moves slowly and quietly toward the animal. It's important for the hunter to be quiet until they're close enough to shoot. Stand hunters stay in one place and hide while waiting for an animal to walk by. This method works well near an area that's known to have animals pass through or feed.

WILD FILE

Scat is animal waste. Hunters should know how to identify the scat of different animals.

Stand hunters might wait for an animal, like this deer, near a popular feeding area.

Fowling for Fun

Do you want to go fowling? That's hunting for birds, which are also called fowl. Hunters use either guns or traps to go fowling. People hunt two kinds of birds—waterfowl and upland game birds.

Hunters almost always use shotguns when hunting upland birds, like turkeys.

Waterfowl are birds that spend most of their time in or around water. Waterfowl include ducks and geese. Hunters have to hide in blinds while hunting waterfowl. That's because waterfowl have excellent vision and can see color better than people can. There are different kinds of blinds for different kinds of hunting.

Upland game birds spend most of their time on land. These birds include turkeys, pheasant, grouse, partridge, and quail. Hunters who are fowling upland game birds need to be very quiet. That's because these birds have a great sense of hearing.

WILD FILE

Hunting blinds cover hunters so animals can't see them. Some blinds are like pop-up tents or sleeping bags, while others are a **permanent** box with windows.

Hunter's Best Friend

Who's a hunter's best friend? A dog, of course. Hunters use several breeds for hunting, such as beagles, Cocker spaniels, and English pointers. These dogs can keep a hunter company. They also have special skills. Different breeds are good at retrieving, pointing, and flushing.

Retrieving dogs know how to collect game after it's been shot. They can return the game to the hunter. Retrieving dogs include golden retrievers and Labrador retrievers. Pointing dogs know how to point, or freeze in a certain position, toward a bird. Then, the hunter knows where to point. Pointing dogs include Britanny's and English setters. Flushing dogs creep through ground cover to scare birds from hiding. Then, the hunter can see them. A springer spaniel is an example of a good flushing dog.

This hunting dog has special skills. It can retrieve game for its owner—without eating it.

Bows and Arrows

Not all hunters use guns. Some use bows and arrows. This form of hunting can be more peaceful and relaxing. Hunters can use a bow and arrows to bag both small and big game. However, it's not easy! It takes practice and lots of patience to use a bow and arrows for hunting.

You have a few bows to choose from—long bows, recurve bows, and compound bows. Long bows are simple and classic with a straight **limb**, while recurve bows have a curved limb. Compound bows are the most common bow used by hunters today. They are **complex** bows, with a fast shot. They can shoot an arrow at up to 350 feet (106.7 m) per second.

WILD FILE

Cross bows are designed to be shot almost like a gun.

You have to be very quiet as you sneak up to your game, because arrows have to be shot at a closer range than guns.

Respect for Nature

Many hunters have a deep respect for nature and animals. They can help keep animal populations in check by hunting a certain number and **species** of animal.

How does hunting help the **environment**? Every ecosystem has a food web, or a transfer of energy from plants to animals to other animals. The balance in an ecosystem can be thrown off by rough weather, predators, sicknesses, and overpopulation. If too many animals of one kind live in one area, this can upset the food chain.

Special groups in each state keep track of game animal populations. The hunting season for each animal is carefully decided based on the number of animals in the area. An animal may be hunted only during its hunting season, and only a certain number can be hunted.

Many hunters are conservationists. That means they want to protect the environment.

Time to Go!

Do you want to go hunting? It takes knowledge, skills, patience, and practice. However, hunting can be a great activity that allows you to spend time outdoors and learn from experienced hunters. You can learn important skills for surviving in nature, from observing your surroundings to navigating trails to knowing animal behaviors.

Learning wilderness skills will make you a better hunter. Keep your eyes open for animal tracks or birds flying overhead. Check your direction on a compass and pay attention to landmarks. Listen carefully for animals. You might hear a duck calling or a deer leaping through the brush. These clues can get you in tune with your natural surroundings and ready to hunt in the wilderness. Time to go hunting!

SAFETY TIPS

- Take a hunter safety course before you go hunting.
- Keep an eye out for other hunters in your area.
- Hunting is a serious sport. Never hunt with someone who is playing around or not following safety rules.
- Get familiar with your weapon at a target shooting range before you hunt.
- Keep the safety on your gun while carrying it.
- Only handle guns under adult supervision—and always assume a gun is loaded.
- Never lean your gun against something. If it falls, it could fire.
- Never point a gun at anything but your target—and never play around with it.
- Only shoot if you can clearly identify your target.
- Wear the right clothing for your hunting trip. Bright orange clothes help other hunters recognize you in the woods.

Keep an eye out for animal tracks as you hunt. Hunting can help you learn to be a part of nature.

GLOSSARY

ancient: Very old.

behavior: The way a person or animal acts.

complex: Having many parts.

ecosystem: A natural community of living and nonliving things.

environment: The conditions that surround a living thing and affect the way it lives.

generation: A group of individuals born about the same time.

habitat: The natural home for plants, animals, and other living things.

harvest: To gather, catch, hunt, or kill something for human use, sport, or population control.

license: An official paper giving someone the right to do something.

limb: The curved, hard part of a bow.

lottery: A drawing of lots used to decide something.

permanent: Lasting or meant to last for a long time.

reservation: Having something held for one's use.

species: A kind of living thing.

FOR MORE INFORMATION

Books

Carpenter, Tom. *Duck Hunting*. Lake Elmo, MN: Focus Readers, 2018.

Moran, Shelby. *We're Going Deer Hunting*. New York, NY: PowerKids Press, 2017.

Websites

Animal Tracks
www.maine.gov/sos/kids/about/wildlife/tracks
Check out these animal tracks before you go hunting.

Hunting Facts for Kids
kids.kiddle.co/Hunting
Learn more about hunting throughout history.

Publisher's note to educators and parents: Our editors have carefully reviewed these websites to ensure that they are suitable for students. Many websites change frequently, however, and we cannot guarantee that a site's future contents will continue to meet our high standards of quality and educational value. Be advised that students should be closely supervised whenever they access the Internet.

INDEX